PEGASUS ACTIVE READING

WORLD'S GREAT AUTHORS

Compiled and Edited by
Tapasi De

CONTENT

1. Introduction 4

2. William Shakespeare 5

3. Charles Dickens 29

4. Rabindranath Tagore 40

5. Sir Arthur Ignatius Conan Doyle 53

6. Mark Twain 65

7. Enid Blyton 75

8. J.K. Rowling 85

9. Lewis Carroll 95

10. Agatha Christie 104

Introduction

The world of literature is a huge one. It is full of varied books, articles, diaries, plays, letters, biographies, and many other kinds of fictional and non-fictional writings. People who contribute to this immensely rich and varied field generally have rich minds and even richer imagination. They maybe thought and of course they are, much above the ordinary lot who lead a mundane life seldom leaving a mark in this world.

These special people called 'authors' have made significant contribution to the world they live in by their writings, over the decades. They have entertained people irrespective of their age; they have awakened awareness regarding various social issues; they have also brought tremendous political changes when monarchy collapsed and democracy came in! Such is the magic and power of these specially gifted people.

This book Greatest Authors has been created with a purpose. The purpose is simple; to enlighten young children about some of the greatest authors of all times who are extremely talented and who do not fail to interest us even in the modern era! To also let the young readers know about their contribution to the world of literature and of couse to society.

WILLIAM SHAKESPEARE

William Shakespeare was an English poet and playwright, universally acknowledged to be the greatest writer in English language and the world's pre-eminent dramatist. He is often called England's national poet and the 'Bard of Avon'.

It is indeed strange that though Shakespeare is recognized as one of literature's greatest influences, very little is actually known about him. Whatever we know about his life comes from the registrar records, court records, wills, marriage certificates and his tombstone.

Early Life

William Shakespeare was born in Stratford-on-Avon, the son of John Shakespeare, a glove maker and dealer in wool. John was a prominent man in Stratford. By 1560, he was one of the fourteen members who formed the town council. William's mother was Mary Arden who was the youngest daughter in her family. She inherited much of her father's landowning and farming estate when he died. William was the third child of John and Mary Shakespeare.

Shakespeare's birthplace in Stratford

Shakespeare probably attended Stratford Grammar School in his childhood. When he was 18, he married Anne Hathaway in 1582. At that time Anne was 26. After sometime their daughter, Susanna, was born. It is generally thought that Skakespeare must have been in Stratford when Hamnet and Judith, his other two children were born in 1585.

Between the years 1580 and 1592, what Shakespeare did is unknown because no records of his life and works exist of that period. This period of time is often referred to as the 'lost years'. It is possible that he spent this entire period in London after leaving Stratford to escape a charge of deer poaching in a park belonging to Sir Thomas Lucy of Charlecote, near Stratford. Some records say that he was employed at a playhouse 'in a very mean rank' during this time. Researchers make assumptions that during these 'lost years', Shakespeare might have tended horses for theatergoers or worked as a sailor, a teacher or a coachman. Some think that he might have been a soldier, a law clerk, a theater page, or a moneylender. He could have held several of these jobs or he may have held none of them!

Researcher *a person who carefully investigates and studies about something*
Moneylender *a person who lends money at interest*

World's Great Authors

Shakespeare may also have spent the time travelling to far off towns or even to foreign countries. His plays suggest that he visited Italy, for more than a dozen of them including *The Merchant of Venice, Romeo and Juliet, All's Well That Ends Well, Othello, Coriolanus, Julius Caesar, The Two Gentlemen of Verona, The Taming of the Shrew, Titus Andronicus, Much Ado About Nothing,* and *The Winter's Tale*—all have scenes set in Italy.

Career

How Shakespeare first started his career in the theatre no one knows for certain. Whether an acting troupe recruited Shakespeare in his hometown or he was forced on his own to travel to London to begin his career, is not clearly known. In the year 1592 came the first reference to Shakespeare in the world of the theatre. The dramatist Robert Greene declared in his death-bed autobiography that, *'There is an upstart crow, beautified with our feathers, that with his Tygers heart wrapt in a Players hide supposes he is as well able to bombast out a blank verse as the best of you; and, being an absolute Johannes Factotum, is in his*

Troupe *a group of dancers, actors, or other entertainers who travel*
Autobiography *an statement of a person's life written by that person himself*

own conceit the only Shake-scene in a country'. After Greene's death, his editor, Henry Chettle, publicly apologized to Shakespeare in the Preface to his 'Kind-Heart's Dream' for this rude comment made by Greene.

While in London, Shakespeare lived alone in rented accommodations while his wife and children remained in Stratford. Why his family did not move to London with him is unknown. At that time, entrepreneurs built theatres and competed for audiences with the best writers of the age. This included not only Shakespeare but also stalwarts like Christopher Marlowe and Ben Jonson.

In 1592, when an epidemic of plague closed the theatres, the versatile Shakespeare wrote sonnets and other poetry until the theatres reopened in 1594. The same year, he joined a newly formed drama group called the Lord Chamberlain's Men, serving there as a writer and an actor. During this time, England prospered under the reign of Elizabeth. There was peace and prosperity all around. Women as well as men could speak their minds on important issues of the day; perhaps they were inspired by their outspoken queen. Many of

Versatile *many-sided*
Entrepreneurs *a person who starts a business to make profit*
Epidemic *the taking place of an infectious disease on a large scale at a particular time*

Shakespeare's women characters reflect this trait of mental strength.

Shakespeare produced most of his well-known works between 1589 and 1613. His early plays were mainly comedies and histories, the literary genre which he raised to the peak of artistic sophistication by the end of the 16th century. He then wrote mainly tragedies until about 1608, including Hamlet, King Lear, Othello, and Macbeth, all of which are considered to be the finest works in the English language. In the last years of his career, he wrote tragicomedies, also known as romances, and collaborated with other playwrights.

Though, today it is an established fact that Shakespeare was a highly talented poet and playwright in his own times, but his reputation did not rise to its present heights until the 19th century. The Romantics, in particular, recognised Shakespeare's genius, and the Victorians worshipped Shakespeare with deep reverence. His plays remain highly popular even till today and are constantly studied and performed.

Playwright *a person who composes plays*
reputation *the opinions that generally people have about something or somebody*

Criticism

Elizabethan era had numerous dramatists who excelled in their work. The popularity of theatre and the competition between playwrights in England culminated into a 'golden age of drama'. This golden age produced some of the most important works in English literature. Dramatists like Thomas Kyd, Christopher Marlowe, Ben Jonson, Francis Beaumont and John Fletcher were all significant figures of the age producing some of the finest works of all times.

In such a productive and fertile age came Shakespeare who quickly rose to such importance in his profession that he provoked attacks from disappointed rivals. In 1592, Robert Greene, one of his influential contemporaries accused him of plagiarism, which plainly showed that envy dictated the attack. The pamphlet containing this accusation was published after Greene's death which provoked a lot of criticism.

Shakespeare's works are the greatest representation of art from Elizabethan England. They cover the economic, social, and educational aspects of

---

Contemporaries *living or happening at the same time*
Accused *a person who is charged with a crime*
Plagiarism *the practice of reproducing someone else's work and claiming them to be one's own*

the age. No other art form, including painting, could provide so much information about life in Elizabethan England. Not only can we see and observe what went on, but we can view the ideas, language, and thoughts as well through words and actions.

Theatre in Shakespeare's Times

During the age of Shakespeare, all plays which were written had to be approved by the government's censor. This is because plays at that time were considered morally or politically offensive and could be banned. It was considered so very offensive that many a time the playwright would be imprisoned too.

Shakespeare presented his plays at inns, courtyards, royal palaces, private residences, playhouses and the Globe Theatre built in 1599. The playhouses in Shakespeare's time were wooden structures with tiers of seating galleries in the shape of a horseshoe. They could seat two thousand to three thousand people who paid two or more pennies. It is believed that at that time the theatre lovers who were wealthy could pay extra to sit on the stage!

The main floor, which was surrounded by the galleries, had no roof and no seats. A person could stand and watch the play by paying a penny. This area was called a 'pit'. Up to one thousand people could stand and watch performances in this area under a hot sun or dark clouds.

The stage of the Globe theatre was four to six feet above ground level. There was no curtain that opened or closed at the beginning or at the end of the plays. A wall with two or three doors leading to the dressing rooms of the actors stood at the back of the stage. These rooms collectively were known as the 'tiring house'.

Males played all the characters, even that of women! Actors played gods, ghosts, demons, and other supernatural characters. They could pop up from the underworld through a trap door on the stage or descend down to Earth from heaven on a winch line from the ceiling. The sound of thunder was created off stage, by beating a sheet metal. To demonstrate that an actor had suffered a fencing wound, he simply had to slap his hand against a pouch beneath his shirt to release 'blood' showing his death.

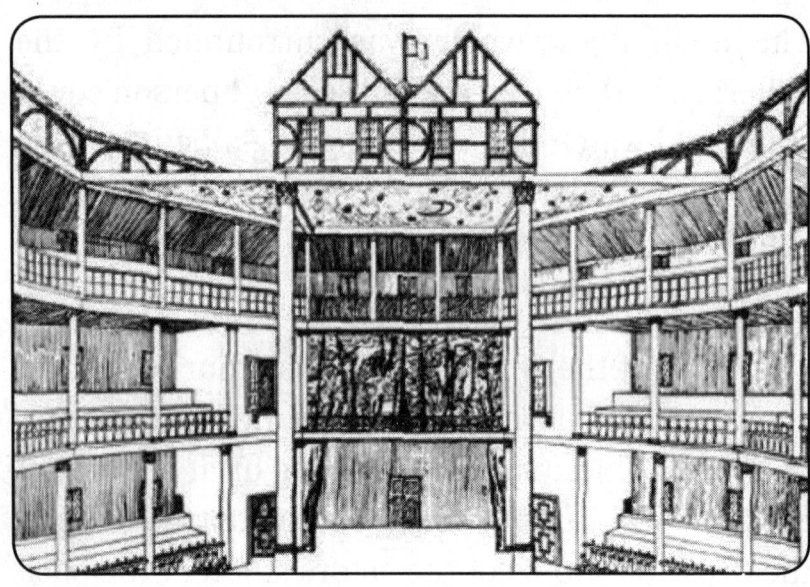

Globe Theatre

Globe Theatre

Although Shakespeare's plays were performed at different venues during the playwright's career, the Globe Theatre in the Southwark district of London was the place at which his best known plays were first performed. The Globe was built during Shakespeare's early period in 1599 by one of his long-standing associates, Cuthbert Burbage.

The theater that Cuthbert Burbage built had a total capacity between 2,000 and 3,000 spectators. Due to the absence of electric lights, all performances at the Globe were conducted during the day (probably in the mid-afternoon spanning between 2 p.m. and 5 p.m.). As most of the stage of the Globe theatre was open air and the apparatus for sound system were poor, the actors were compelled to shout their lines, stress their intonations, and engage themselves in exaggerated theatrical gestures. The plays which were staged at the Globe were completely devoid of background scenery although costumes and props were utilized. There was no proscenium arch, no curtains, and no stagehands than the actors themselves. Instead, changes of scenes were suggested in the speeches and narrative situations of the plays.

End of Globe Theatre

The original structure of the Globe Theatre existed until June 29, 1613, when its thatched roof was set on fire by a cannon fired during the performance of the play Henry VIII. The Globe burned to ashes and could not be saved. At this time, Shakespeare had almost retired and was at Stratford-on-Avon where he died three years later at the age of fifty-two.

The Globe was reconstructed in the year 1614, when tiles replaced the straw on its partial

Intonations *the rising and falling of ones voice while talking*
Exaggerated *to overstate beyond normal*
Proscenium arch *an arch framing the opening between the stage and the auditorium in theatres*

roof. In 1642, however, a quarter-century after Shakespeare's death, again an anti-theater regime assumed power in England and closed down all of the country's theaters. Two years later, Cromwell's followers destroyed the Globe, demolished the site and constructed slum dwelling housing upon it.

Works of Shakespeare

Shakespeare was the most popular playwright of London in the Elizabethan Era. With the passage of centuries, his genius eclipsed all others of his age, Jonson, Marlowe, Kyd, Greene, Dekker, Heywood. None could surpass the excellence of the Bard's

A scene from Shakespeare's play, *King Lear*

work. He created the most vivid characters of the Elizabethan stage. His usage of language, both lofty and low, shows a remarkable wit and subtlety. The most striking feature of his themes are that they are so universal that they have transcended generations and have become timeless.

Shakespeare's works can be generally divided into four periods.

The *first* period has its roots in the Roman and medieval drama. The earliest plays of Shakespeare owe a debt to Christopher Marlowe, whose writing probably gave much inspiration at the outset of his career.

The *second* period showed more growth in style, and the construction becoming less laboured and more natural. The histories of this period are Shakespeare's best. They portrayed the lives of kings and royalty. It is during this period that he begins the interweaving of comedy and tragedy, which were to become the important genres of his work.

The *third* period is known for the great tragedies which he created. These were the principal works

---

Genres *a category of art, music, or literature*

which earned Shakespeare his fame in the later centuries. Shakespeare is at his best in these tragedies. The comedies of this period, however, show Shakespeare at literary crossroads—moody and without the clear comic resolution of the previous comedies.

The *fourth* period encompasses romantic tragicomedy. Shakespeare in this period which was the last phase of his career, seemed to be preoccupied with themes of redemption. The writing is more serious yet more lyrical and symbolic.

Genres of Shakespeare's Plays

Most of the Elizabethan plays can be divided into several genres. These divisions were derived from the plays of ancient Greek and Roman times.

Tragedy

Tragedies are plays with very serious themes dealing with the sorrow and the downfall of a superior character due to some flaw in his character. Shakespeare wrote many tragedies throughout his career and one of his earliest tragedy was the Titus

---

Redemption *the action of saving or being saved from a sin or error*
Genres *a category of art, music, or literature*

A scene from *Merchant of Venice*

Andronicus. But his most popular tragedies are the ones written between 1601 and 1608. These include his four major tragedies—*Hamlet, Othello, King Lear* and *Macbeth*. There are also plays which can be considered love tragedies, such as *Romeo and Juliet, Antony & Cleopatra* and *Othello*.

Here is a list of Shakespearean tragedies:
- *Romeo and Juliet*
- *Macbeth*
- *King Lear*
- *Hamlet*
- *Othello*

- *Titus Andronicus*
- *The Tragedy of Julius Caesar*
- *Antony and Cleopatra*
- *Coriolanus*
- *The History of Troilus and Cressida*
- *The Life of Timon of Athens*
- *Cymbeline*

Comedy

Comedies are dramatic works in which the central motif is the triumph over adverse circumstance, resulting in a successful or happy conclusion. A lighthearted style occurred through the entire play. Shakespearean comedies often had the following features which resulted in their comic fun.

- *A struggle of young lovers to overcome difficulty that is often presented by elders*
- *Separation and unification*
- *Mistaken identities*
- *A clever servant*
- *Heightened tensions, often within a family*
- *Multiple, intertwining plots*
- *Use of puns*

Some of his remarkable comedies are *As you like, Midsummer Nights Dream* and *Merchant of Venice*

A further subcategory of the comedy is the tragicomedy, a serious play with a happy ending.

History

Shakespeare wrote many plays based on the lives of English kings. Shakespeare lived during the reign of Queen Elizabeth I, the last monarch in the house of the Tudors. So his history plays are often regarded as Tudor propaganda by critics.

Here is a list of Shakespeare's historical plays:
- *King John*
- *Edward III*
- *Richard II*
- *Henry IV, Part 1*
- *Henry IV, Part 2*
- *Henry V*
- *Henry VI, Part 1*
- *Henry VI, Part 2*
- *Henry VI, Part 3*

- Richard III (also considered a tragedy)
- *Henry VIII*
- *Sir Thomas More*

Romance

Critics and scholars often think that Shakespeare's plays can have a fourth genre, namely the romance. Some of the features of romances were a redemptive plotline with a happy ending, use of magic and other fantastical elements, and a mixture of 'civilized' and 'pastoral' scenes as in *The Tempest*

Shakespeare's romance plays include:
- *Pericles, Prince of Tyre*
- *Cymbeline*
- *The Winter's Tale*
- *The Tempest*
- *The Two Noble Kinsmen*

Sonnets of Shakespeare

A sonnet is a fourteen-line lyric poem, traditionally written in iambic pentameter. Shakespeare had written 154 sonnets dealing with themes such as the passage of time, love, beauty and mortality.

They were first published in a quarto in 1609.

The majority of the sonnets are addressed to a young man, with whom the poet had an intense romantic relationship. The poet spends the first seventeen sonnets trying to convince the young man to marry and have children so that the children will look just like their father ensuring his immortality.

The final sonnets are addressed to a lascivious and scheming woman known to modern readers as the 'dark lady'.

Main Sources of Shakespeare's Works

Shakespeare used a variety of sources for his plays.

One of the prime sources of Shakespeare was **Giovanni Boccacio**, the Italian prose and poetry writer of the mid 14th century. His Decameron forms the source for Shakespeare's plays like *All's Well That Ends Well, Cymbeline* and *The Two Gentlemen of Verona*.

Lascivious having an extra sexual interest or desire
Scheming making secret plans

Critics have reason to believe that Shakespeare also worked from **Arthur Brooke's** poem entitled *The Tragical History of Romeus and Juliet* for his famous tragedy *Romeo and Juliet*.

In around 1200 AD, **Saxo Grammaticus** the Danish historian wrote *Gesta Danorum* (Deeds of the Danes) which talked about the Kings of Denmark. It narrated the story of **Amleth**. It is accepted universally now that Shakespeare's well-known tragedy *The Tragedy of Hamlet, Prince of Denmark* is based on this chronicle.

Raphael Holinshed's Chronicles recorded the history of England, Scotland and Ireland. This became Shakespeare's primary source for his historical plays. It should be noted that Shakespeare did not set out to create historically accurate accounts. He reshaped history for dramatic purposes.

Plutarch, the ancient-Greek historian and philosopher became the main source for Shakespeare's Roman plays. Plutarch created a text called *Parallel Lives* that contains over forty biographies of Greek and Roman leaders. This became the source for plays like *Antony and*

Chronicle *a factual written record of important or historical events in the order of their occurrence*

Cleopatra, Coriolanus, Julius Caesar and *Timon of Athens.*

Female Characters in Shakespeare's Plays

Gender roles during the Elizabethan era were clearly defined, with men being superior to women. Men had a great influence on women. While a man went out to work, a woman at that time was only expected to stay at home and manage the household duties. The women of the Elizabethan era were given education only if they were members of the nobility. Otherwise, they had to stay at home and learn household chores. For the women of noble birth, education included knowledge of several languages, including Latin, Greek, Italian, and French. However, even noblewomen were not allowed to go to universities and were only taught by tutors at home.

Shakespeare's plays have shown some remarkable female characters who stand out in their own right. They tell us a lot about the status of women in Shakespeare's time and his opinion about them. The female characters can be categorized into the following categories.

The indecent Woman

These characters are cheeky and flirtatious. They are often characters from the working class such as the Nurse in *Romeo and Juliet,* Margaret in *Much Ado about Nothing* or Audrey in *As you Like It.*

The Innocent, Tragical Woman

These women are often pure and chaste at the beginning of the play, and tragically die once their innocence is lost. Shakespeare's treatment of these young innocent women is quite insensitive. These characters are generally courtly, high born characters such as Juliet from *Romeo and Juliet,* Lavinia from *Titus Andronicus* or Ophelia from *Hamlet.* Their high social position makes their death seem all the more tragic.

The Scheming Femme Fatale

Lady Macbeth is the model femme fatale. Her manipulation of Macbeth inevitably leads them to their deaths. In her ambition to become the Queen, she encourages her husband to murder the King. In the play *King Lear,* his daughters, Goneril and Regan, plot to inherit their father's fortune. Once

---

Flirtatious *a behaviour that suggests a playful sexual attraction towards someone*
Manipulation *the act of managing something skilfully*

again, their ambition leads them to their deaths.

The Humorous Unmarriable Woman

Katherine from *The Taming of the Shrew* is a prime example of the witty, but unmarriable woman. These women are presented as clever, bold and independent. But they are put in their place by the end of the play.

The 'Married off' Woman

Many of Shakespeare's comedies end with an eligible woman being married off. These women are often very young and they are passed from their father's care to their new husband's. Mostly, these are high-born characters such as Miranda in *The Tempest* who is married to Ferdinand, Helena and Hermia in *A Midsummer Night's Dream* and Hero in *Much Ado about Nothing*.

Women Disguised as Men

Rosalind in *As You Like it and* Viola *in Twelfth Night* both dress as men. Consequently, they are able to play a more active role in the play's narrative. It has been observed that as 'men', these characters have more freedom, highlighting the lack of social liberty for women in Shakespeare's time.

Falsely Accused of Adultery

Women in Shakespeare's plays are sometimes wrongly accused of adultery and suffer greatly as a result. For example, Desdemona is killed by Othello who suspects her infidelity. Again, Hero *in Much Ado about Nothing* falls terribly ill when she is falsely accused by Claudio. It seems that Shakespeare's women are judged by their femininity even when they remain faithful to their husbands and husbands-to-be.

Death of Shakespeare

Shakespeare spent the last five years of his life in Stratford. By then, he was a wealthy man. He died on April 23, 1616 and was buried in Holy Trinity Church in Stratford.

Infidelity disloyalty

CHARLES DICKENS

Charles Dickens, the English author continues to be one of the most widely read Victorian novelists till today. He is remembered for his immortal characters like David Copperfield, Oliver Twist, and Nicholas Nickelby who remain familiar characters even today. His novels describe the life and conditions of the poor and working class in the Victorian era of England, when people lived by strict rules.

Early Days

Charles John Huffam Dickens was born on February 7, 1812, at Portsea (later part of Portsmouth) on the southern coast of England, to John and Elizabeth Dickens. Charles was the second child amongst the eight children. His father was a pay clerk in the navy office. At the age of 12, there was a dramatic turn in the life of young Charles. His father, unable to pay his large debts, was packed off to the Marshalsea Debtors' Prison in London. Within a few days, the rest of the family went to live near the debtor's prison except Charles. Young Charles had to earn his living alone, washing bottles at Warren's Blacking Factory. Young Charles had to work with the working class people. This experience proved so shocking and humiliating to the little boy that it haunted him for the rest of his life. This experience of lonely hardship was the most significant event of his life. It formed his view of the world and would later be described in a number of his novels.

It can be quoted in the writer's own words —'*No words can express the secret agony of my soul...I felt my early hopes of growing up to be a learned and distinguished man crushed in my breast.*'

Though soon the young boy was re-united with his family, the previous easy life enjoyed by Charles never came back. Charles returned to school when his father received an inheritance and was able to repay his debts. But in 1827, at age fifteen, he had to leave school again and work as an office boy.

The very next year, he became a freelance reporter and stenographer at the law courts of London. By 1832 he had become a reporter for two London newspapers. A year later, he began to contribute a series of impressions and sketches to other newspapers and magazines, signing some of them as 'Boz'. These contributions describing the scenes of London life went far to establish his reputation. They were published in 1836 as *Sketches by Boz*, his first book. Based on this success Charles married Catherine Hogarth from whom he had ten children.

Family of Dickens

Inheritance *getting something from the predecessors*
Stenographer *a person who writes in shorthand and types it on a typewriter*

Works of his Early Period

The Posthumous Papers of the Pickwick Club was the first novel of Dickens which he began publishing in monthly installments, in the year 1836. It speaks of the Pickwick Club of London, headed by Samuel Pickwick who decide to establish a travelling society in which four members journey about England and make reports on their travels. Publishing in installments had become the standard method of writing and producing fiction in the Victorian period. Dickens' Pickwick Papers became a roaring success. It became one of the most popular works of the time, and continued to be so after it was published in the book form in 1837.

After Pickwick's success, Dickens began publishing his new novel, *Oliver Twist*. At that time, he was also the editor of *Bentley's Miscellany*, a new monthly magazine. He continued publishing his novel in his later magazines. *Oliver Twist* clearly portrays Dickens's interest in the life of the slums as it traced the fortunes and misfortunes of an innocent orphan through the streets of London. Though Dickens was immensely successful as a writer, for the next decade, his books did not achieve the standard of his early successes. Such works include *Nicholas Nickleby, The Old Curiosity Shop and Barnaby Rudge.*

In 1842 Dickens, went on a five-month lecture tour of the United States. The level of his popularity was equally high in America as it was in his own land! On his return he wrote *American Notes*, a book that criticizes American life as being culturally backward and materialistic. Some of the novels which were published after this time were *Martin Chuzzlewi , A Christmas Carol and The Chimes.*

First Major Novels

After a year of stay in Italy and writing *Pictures from Italy* in 1846, Dickens published *Dealings with the Firm of Dombey and Son* in installments which continued till 1848. This completed novel established a new standard in the Dickensian novel. This also marked the turning point in his career. It depicts a sombre view of England, and this tone becomes a characteristic of Dickens's future novels.

Dickens's next novel, *David Copperfield*, was a remarkable literary work. It is the first complete record of a young man's life in Victorian England. Universally acclaimed as an autobiographical novel, this novel has fictionalized elements of Dickens's childhood, his career of journalism and his love life. Though Copperfield is not Dickens's greatest novel, but it was his personal favourite.

In 1850, Dickens began a new magazine, *Household Words*. His editorials and articles were based upon English politics, social institutions and family life. This weekly magazine ran till 1859, when Dickens began to publish a new weekly, *All the Year Round*. In both these periodicals he published some of his major novels.

Dark Novels of a Dark Phase

During the 1850s there was dark and sad phase in Dickens's life. In 1851, within a period of two weeks, Dickens's father and one of his daughters

Periodicals *a magazine or newspaper which is published at regular intervals*

died. In 1858, a year after he fell in love with an actress, and separated from his wife. Partly due to the sudden deaths, critics often call Dickens's next series of works as his 'dark' novels, though they are considered to be some of the finest pieces of fiction till date. Some of them were *Bleak House and Hard Times*. Also written during this time, *Little Dorrit* maybe regarded as Dickens's greatest novel. In it, he portrays the conditions of England as he saw it. The novel also portrays the conflict between the world's harshness and human values in its most impressive artistic form.

Later Works

In the later period of his career, Dickens gave public readings from his novels, which became even more popular than his lectures. In 1859 Dickens published *A Tale of Two Cities*, a historical novel about the French Revolution. His next novel, *Great Expectations* is regarded by some as his most perfectly executed work of art. It is the story of a young man's moral development from childhood to adult life. Three years later he published *Our*

Mutual Friend, which provides the readers with an insight of how he viewed London.

In 1865, Dickens met with a railroad accident from which he did not recover. He tired himself out by continuing to travel throughout the British Isles and America to read before audiences. Dickens died of a fatal stroke on June 9, 1870, leaving the novel, *The Mystery of Edwin Drood*, unfinished. The day of his burial was made a day of national mourning in England. Contrary to his wish to be buried in Rochester Cathedral, he was buried in the Poets' Corner of Westminster Abbey.

Literary Style of Dickens

Dickens was gifted with a style marked by satire and extraordinary literary genius. He worked intensively on developing arresting names for his characters that would help the storyline to develop. For example, the name Mr. Murdstone in *David Copperfield* conjures up twin allusions to 'murder' and stony coldness. Dickens's literary style is also a mixture of fantasy and realism. Some typical features of Dickens's style have been given below.

Autobiographical Elements

It is a common phenomenon that authors frequently draw their literary characters from people they have known in real life. *David Copperfield* is regarded as strongly autobiographical. Dickens's experiences as a law clerk and court reporter, his bitter experience at the Blacking factory, Dickens's father being sent to prison for debt, became a common theme in many of his books. Lucy Stroughill, a childhood sweetheart may have influenced Dickens's portrayal of girls in many of his novels.

Writing in Episodes

Most of Dickens's major novels were first written in monthly or weekly installments in journals such as *Master Humphrey's Clock and Household Words*. Later he got them reprinted in the book form. These installments made the stories cheap and accessible.

Social Commentary

Dickens's novels always acted as the mirrors of the society. They were commentaries on the contemporary society. He was a fierce critic of the poverty and social stratification of the Victorian society. Dickens's second novel, *Oliver Twist* still shocks the readers with its images of poverty and crime.

Literary Techniques

Dickens is often described as using 'idealised' characters and highly sentimental scenes to contrast with his caricatures and the ugly social truths. In *Oliver Twist*, Dickens provides the readers with an idealised portrait of a boy who was unrealistically so 'good' that his values never fell even when in contact with evil. This idealism serves only to highlight Dickens's goal of giving a passionate social commentary.

Use of Coincidence

Dickens's novels many a time show strange occurrences of coincidences. Oliver Twist turns out to be the lost nephew of the upper-class family that randomly rescues him from the dangers of the pickpocket group.

Caricatures a picture or a description of a person to create a comic effect

What do Critics Say?

Critics are of the opinion that Dickens's novels combine brutality with fairy-tale fantasy; sharp reality with romance, and the ordinary with the strange. Dickens himself believed that his novels had a moral purpose—to arouse moral sentiments in the readers and to encourage virtuous behaviour.

RABINDRANATH TAGORE

Rabindranath Tagore, the Nobel laureate was a multitalented personality. He was a Bengali poet, an artist, a Brahmo Samaj philosopher, a novelist, a playwright, a painter and a composer—all combined into one. Rabindranath Tagore started composing art works at a very tender age.

Even though he is mainly known as a poet, his multifaceted talent shone in many genres of art such as, novels, short stories, dramas, articles, essays, painting etc. He was a social reformer, a patriot and above all, a great humanitarian and a philosopher. The national anthems of India and Bangladesh have been taken from his composition.

Early Life and Childhood

Rabindranath Tagore was born on May 7, 1861 in Jorasanko (Tagore House), Kolkata, India. He was the fourteenth child of Debendranath Tagore and Sarada Devi. Tagore's grandfather was a social reformer and a wealthy landowner. The Tagores were a progressive and wealthy family. Their home was a hub of social activity and culture and they often hosted theatrical and musical performances in their mansion. Many of the Tagore children succeeded as authors, poets, musicians, and civil servants.

Tagore's childhood days were mostly confined to the family estate under the watchful eye of servants. After failing to succeed in the conventional school system, Rabindranath obtained his early education from tutors who taught him at home. He studied a wide array of subjects including art, history, science, mathematics, Bengali, Sanskrit, and English, Hindu Scriptures Upanishads, Romantic poetry like that of Percy Bysshe Shelley and classical poetry of Kālidāsa.

Upanishads each of a series of Hindu sacred texts written in Sanskrit

Tagore and his children

At the age of twenty-two, on December 9, 1883, Tagore married Bhabatarini, later known as Mrinalini Devi. They had five children. They were daughters Madhurilata, Renuka, Mira and sons called Rathindra and Samindranath. In 1890, Tagore moved to the vast family estate in Shilaidaha, a region now part of present Bangladesh. His wife and children joined him in 1898. He travelled by a barge throughout the rural region among the Padma River's sandy estuaries, collecting rents from the tenants. Tagore was greatly charmed by their pastoral life, the working in the rice fields, watching the fishermen with their nets, visiting school children, and attending feasts in his honour.

The period when he was travelling with his family gained him much inspiration from the people and the landscape. This became a prolific period of writing for him. At this time, he composed works like *Chitra* (A Play in One Act), *Manasi* (The Ideal One), *and Sonar Tari (The Golden Boat).*

Early Works

Tagore began writing poetry at a very early age. Some poems were published anonymously or under his pen name *Bhanusingha*. He soon became a regular contributor to various magazines. His first collection *Kabi Kahini* (Tale of a Poet) was published in 1878. He also started writing short stories.

At the age of thirteen, Tagore went with his father

Anonymously *unknown of anybody's name*

to various parts of India. Then, with the intent to become a barrister, he was off to England to attend the University College in London. But he did not finish his degree. He wrote one of his most famous poems during these years, *Nirjharer Swapnabhanga* (The Fountain Awakened from its Dream).

When Tagore's wife died just one year after the founding of Shantiniketan, he wrote the poems in *Smaran* (In Memoriam). Other works written or published during this period were *Katha O Kahini* (Tales and Stories), *Naivedya* (poetry), *Kheya* (poetry), *Raja* (play) (The King of the Dark Chamber), *Dak-ghar* (The Post Office), *The Crescent Moon, Gitimalya* (Wreath of Songs), *Songs of Kabîr, Stray Birds, Sadhana: The Realisation of Life,* and *Balaka* (The Flight of Cranes), and the poems *Fruit-Gathering, The Fugitive and The Gardener.*

It is commonly accepted that the modern Bengali language owes a lot to Tagore. It is he who, by his contributions, enriched Bengali literature. His novels are as varied in their themes and are exceptional in their artistic portrayal of characters and situations.

Gitanjali, a Masterpiece

Gitanjali is an illustrious work by Rabindranath Tagore and it echoes the true Indian Philosophy. It is a collection of poems. The original collection of 157 poems in Bengali was published on August 14, 1910. The English *Gitanjali* or *Song Offerings* is a collection of 103 English poems which Tagore translated himself from his Bengali poems. This was first published in November 1912 by the 'India Society of London'. This publication at once became the talk of Europe. English poets were deeply touched. As a result, the greatest literary honour, the Nobel Prize, was awarded to him by the Swedish Academy in 1913. Rabindranath Tagore was suddenly known globally.

The *Gitanjali* contained translations of 53 poems from the original Bengali Gitanjali, and 50 other poems from his drama *Achalayatan* and eight other books of poetry mainly from *Gitimalya, Naivedya* and *Kheya*.

One of the most celebrated poems from *Gitanjali* has been quoted below.

Mind Without Fear

Where the mind is without fear and the head is held high;

Where knowledge is free;

Where the world has not been broken up

into fragments by narrow domestic walls;

Where words come out from the depth of truth;

Where tireless striving stretches its arms towards perfection;

Where the clear stream of reason

has not lost its way into the dreary desert sand of dead habit;

Where the mind is led forward by thee into ever-widening thought and action-

Into that heaven of freedom, my Father, let my country awake.

His Paintings

Rabindranath Tagore started painting in 1924 at the age of 63 years. One of his ardent admirers Victoria Ocampo had noticed with amazement and admiration his paintings during Tagore's visit to Buenos Aires in 1924. She arranged the first exhibition of Tagore's paintings in Paris in May 1930. Later the exhibitions moved to other famous destinations in Europe and America in places like Birmingham, London, Berlin, Munich, Dresden, Copenhagen, Geneva, Moscow, Boston, New York, Phillidelphia and finally in Kolkata in May 1931.

Rabindranath did not have any formal training in art. But with his incomparable genius, he transformed his lack of formal training of art into an advantage and opened new horizons as far as the use of lines and colours. He was prolific in his paintings and sketches producing over 2500 of these within a decade. Over 1500 of them are preserved in Viswa-Bharati, Shantiniketan. The opening of the `Kala Bhavan' by Tagore as a painter was a major contribution in the evolution of Indian art. It was like a landmark in the history of art.

Painting of Tagore

Rabindrasangeet

Rabindranath's extraordinary creative senses and intellect found manifestation in almost every facet of

Manifestation *an indication or presence of something*

fine art. One of the most outstanding amongst them is Rabindrasangeet, which embodies a breathtaking fusion of his sense of music and his poetry. The impact of this unique creation was so great, that it not only withstood the test of time for more than a hundred years, but also secured a unique place for itself in the subcontinent's musical culture!

Indian Classical music and Rabindrasangeet

It is universally accepted that elements of Indian classical music have been used in an extremely intelligent and effective manner in Rabindrasangeet. This forms one of its most significant features. So, many of Tagore's songs partially conform to the ragas of the Indian classical music. In order to create a particular mood to his own satisfaction, he often blended ragas in unexpectedly beautiful and interesting ways.

Contribution in India's Freedom Struggle

Being a humanitarian and a social and religious reformer, Tagore disliked the British Raj ruling over his country. As a patriot, he composed the music and lyrics for India's national anthem—

Humanitarian promoting human welfare

Jana-Gana-Mana. And when Bangladesh became independent in 1971, they chose Tagore's song *Amar Sonar Bangla* (My Golden Bengal) as its national anthem.

When the country needed his support in its freedom struggle, Rabindranath never hesitated to respond. The inspiration which he gave to his countrymen during the political turmoils of 1905 to 1908 is unforgettable. Through his songs, through speeches, through unique literary compositions, through symbolic activities like the Rakhi, he kept alive the national spirit.

In 1911, Bangiya Sahitya Parishad paid him homage on the fiftieth anniversary of his birth,—the first poet to be so honoured.

After the Great War of 1914-18, he severely rebuked the materialism of the West and the ultra nationalism which had led to that war. To the people of Japan, Europe and America, he pointed out the complete absence of noble motives, in their politics, in their economics, and even their religion.

In his own country, he severely criticized the

barbarity, which the English showed at Jalianwala Bagh. He renounced his prestigious 'Knighthood' conferred upon him as a gesture of recognition for his genius.

His contribution in the field of education is remarkable too as he founded Shantiniketan, presently known as the Vishva-Bharati University.

Shantiniketan

The next period of Tagore's life saw the beginning of unique school Shantiniketan (now known as Visva-Bharati University) in 1901. It was built on a part of the family estate lands near Bolpur, West Bengal. Shantiniketan is an experimental school, based on the ashrama model. It emphasises on learning in a harmonious and natural setting. Tagore felt that education using all the five senses and not relying on memorising by rote, was the better way to teach children. Shantiniketan is now a prestigious open air University, a universal meeting place for students from East and West. Its list of alumni includes many notable figures like Indira Gandhi.

Shantiniketan

In 1921, Tagore and agricultural economist Leonard Elmhirst founded the Institute for Rural Reconstruction, Shriniketan (Abode of Peace), near Santiniketan.

Once in a century a man is born with such a rare and many-sided genius as Rabindranath. He enriched all that he touched with the alchemic power of his genius. He was a poet with a unique vision, a painter, and a preacher who gave a new direction to the art and a visionary who could look beyond the barriers of time and place.

Sir Arthur Ignatius Conan Doyle

Sir Arthur Ignatius Conan Doyle was a Scottish medical practitioner and writer. He is well-known for his stories about the detective Sherlock Holmes. These stories are generally considered to be milestones in the field of crime fiction. Doyle was a prolific writer whose other works include science fiction stories, plays, romances, poetry, non-fiction and historical novels.

Birth and Early Years

Arthur Conan Doyle, the creator of the popular detective character Sherlock Holmes, was born in an affluent, strict Irish-Catholic family in Edinburgh, Scotland on May 22, 1859. Although Doyle's family was well-respected in the art world, his father, Charles, had very few achievements. Moreover, he was a life-long alcoholic. Doyle's mother, Mary, on the contrary was a lively and well-educated woman who loved to read. She used to be delighted in telling her young son unusual stories. Her great enthusiasm in weaving wild tales sparked the child's imagination. As Doyle would later recall in his biography, *'In my early childhood, as far as I can remember anything at all, the vivid stories she would tell me stand out so clearly that they obscure the real facts of my life.'*

At the age of 9, Doyle was shipped off to England, where he attended Hodder Place, Stonyhurst—a Jesuit preparatory school from 1868 to 1870. Doyle then went on to study at Stonyhurst College for the next five years. The boarding-school experience was not a happy one for Doyle. Many of his classmates bullied him, and the school practiced ruthless corporal punishment against its students. Over the years, Doyle found consolation in his flair for storytelling, and developed an eager audience of younger students.

Doyle's Medical Career

When Doyle graduated from Stonyhurst College in 1876, his parents expected that he would train himself in the field of some art according to the family's tradition. But they were surprised when he decided to pursue a medical degree at the University of Edinburgh. At the medical college, Doyle met his mentor, Professor Dr Joseph Bell.

Stonyhurst College

Ruthless *having or showing no pity for others*

His keen powers of observation later inspired Doyle to create his much famed fictional detective character, Sherlock Holmes. At the University of Edinburgh, Doyle also had the good fortune to meet his classmates and future fellow authors James Barrie and Robert Louis Stevenson. While studying medicine, Doyle began writing with a short story called *The Mystery of Sasassa Valley*. This was followed by a second story, *The American Tale*, which was published in *London Society*.

When Doyle was in his third year of medical school, he took a ship surgeon's post on a ship sailing for the Arctic Circle. The voyage awakened Doyle's sense of adventure. He depicted this feeling into his work called *Captain of the Pole Star*.

In 1880, Doyle returned to medical school. When he came back at the University of Edinburgh, Doyle became increasingly affected by Spiritualism or 'Psychic religion'. This is a belief system that he would later attempt to spread through a series of his written works. By the time Doyle graduated and received his Bachelor of Medicine degree in 1881, he had already denounced his Roman Catholic faith.

Sir Arthur Ignatius Conan Doyle

Doyle's family

Doyle's first job as a doctor happened when he joined as the medical officer on the steamship called Mayumba, travelling from Liverpool to Africa. After his job on the Mayumba, Doyle settled in Plymouth, England for sometime. When his funds were nearly exhausted, he relocated to Portsmouth and began his first practice.

He spent the next few years struggling to balance his medical career with his efforts to gain recognition as an author. Doyle would later give up medicine altogether, in order to devote all of his attention to his writing and his faith.

Doyle Meets his Wife

In the year 1885, when Doyle was struggling to stabilise himself as a writer, Doyle met and married his first wife, Louisa Hawkins. The couple moved to Upper Wimpole Street and had two children, a daughter and a son. In 1893, Louisa was diagnosed with tuberculosis. While Louisa was ailing, Doyle was attracted to a young woman named Jean Leckie. Louisa ultimately died of tuberculosis in Doyle's arms, in 1906. The following year, Doyle married Jean Leckie, with whom he had two sons and a daughter.

What strikes one most in reviewing Arthur Conan Doyle's personal life is his constant spiritual quest for what is right, what is true, and his valiant attempts to do the right thing.

Career as a Writer

In 1886, Doyle who was struggling to establish himself as an author, started writing the mystery novel *A Tangled Skein*. Two years later, the novel was renamed *A Study in Scarlet* and published in *Beeton's Christmas Annual*. It was A *Study in*

Scarlet, which first introduced the wildly popular characters Detective **Sherlock Holmes** and his assistant, **Dr Watson**. These two immortal characters finally earned Doyle the recognition he had long desired. *A study in Scarlet* was the first among the 60 stories that Doyle wrote based on the character of Sherlock Holmes over the course of his writing career. Also, in 1887, Doyle submitted two letters about his conversion to Spiritualism to a weekly periodical called *Light*.

Doyle vigorously participated in the Spiritualist movement from 1887 to 1916. During this time he wrote three books that experts consider largely autobiographical. These include *Beyond the City, The Stark Munro Letters* and *A Duet with an Occasional Chorus*. The moment Doyle received success as a writer, he decided to retire from medicine. Throughout this period, he also produced a few historical novels like *The Great Shadow*, and his most famous historical novel, *Rodney Stone*.

The extremely productive author that he was, Doyle also composed four of his most popular Sherlock Holmes books during the 1890s and early 1900s.

They were *The Sign of Four, The Adventures of Sherlock Holmes, The Memoirs of Sherlock Holmes* and *The Hounds of Baskervilles*. In 1893, Doyle attempted to kill the character of Sherlock Holmes in order to focus more on writing about Spiritualism. In 1901, however, Doyle reintroduced Sherlock Holmes as a ghost in *The Hounds of Baskervilles* and later brought him back to life in *The Adventure of the Empty House*. Doyle also focused on spreading his faith through a series of written works like *The New Revolution, The Vital Message, The Wanderings of a Spiritualist and History of Spiritualism*.

In 1928, Doyle's final twelve stories about Sherlock Holmes were published in a compilation called *The Casebook of Sherlock Holmes*.

Spiritualism

One of the most striking features of Doyle is his constant spiritual quest for what is **right**, what is **true**, and his valiant attempts to do the right thing. In the early 20th century, Arthur lost many of his relationships. His wife Louisa died of Tuberculosis, his son Kingsley, brother Innes, and many other close relatives succumbed to death one after another. Due to these incidents, Doyle went into a state of depression which turned him into a spiritualist. In 1915 he apparently experienced a conversion to 'psychic religion'. After the war he devoted the rest of his life and career in propagating his new faith through a series of his works like *The New Revelation, The Vital Message, The Wanderings of a Spiritualist (1921), and History of Spiritualism*. From the year 1917 to 1925 he lectured on spiritualism throughout Europe, Australia, the United States, and Canada.

Arthur, as a child, strayed from religious nature for many years. However, by this time he had become increasingly interested and obsessed with spiritualism. He wrote a Professor Challenger novel called *The Land of Mist*. His next book *The Coming of the Fairies*, which he wrote in 1921, supported his views on spiritualism and also *Life beyond life*.

One very practical example can be sighted that Doyle always tried to do the right is when his first wife died after suffering from tuberculosis. For the

Succumbed *unable to resist pressure, temptation or any other negative force*
Obsessed *to fill the mind of someone excessively with something*

last several years of her life, Doyle had been in love with another woman. Yet, he never was unfaithful, until the proper time of mourning was complete. He then married Jean, his second love.

Doyle's Political Career

When the Boer War began, Doyle's energy and patriotic zeal led him to serve as a chief surgeon of a field hospital at Bloemfontein, South Africa, in 1900. His work *The Great Boer War* was widely read and praised for the fairness he expressed regarding both sides. In 1902, he wrote a long pamphlet, *The*

Boar war

War in South Africa: Its Cause and Conduct, to defend the British action in South Africa against widespread criticism by pacifist groups. In August 1902, Doyle received knighthood for his services to England.

Doyle was defeated twice in a bid for a seat in Parliament in 1900 and 1906. In the year 1906, Arthur published *Sir Nigel* a popular historical novel of the Middle Ages. After this, he took up a number of political and humanitarian causes. A few years later he wrote *Divorce Law Reform*, championing equal rights for women in British law, and *The Crime of the Congo*, attacking the exploitation of the colony by Belgium. He also published a second collection of poems, *Songs of the Road*, and began a series of science fiction stories with the novel *The Lost World*, featuring another of his famous characters, Professor Challenger.

After the outbreak of World War I, Doyle organized the Civilian National Reserve against the threat of German invasion. In 1918 he again toured the front lines. These tours, with a number of high-ranking officers, enabled Doyle to write his famous account

Humanitarian *promoting human welfare*

The British Campaigns in France and Flanders, published in six volumes (1916-1919).

Death

Arthur Conan Doyle was diagnosed with Angina Pectoris (Chest pain due to an inadequate supply of oxygen to the heart) which he ignored. On July 7, 1930, Doyle collapsed and died in his house in Crow borough, East Sussex. His last words were directed towards his wife when he said, 'You are wonderful'. And thus ended a brilliant chapter in the world of global literature.

MARK TWAIN

Mark Twain was a renowned American author and humorist. He is a global name due to his novels, *The Adventures of Tom Sawyer* and its sequel, *Adventures of Huckleberry Finn*. The latter is often called 'the Great American Novel'.

Early Years

Samuel L. Clemens who wrote under the pen name of Mark Twain, was born on November 30, 1835, in Florida, Missouri. He was the sixth child of John and Jane Clemens. Mark twain had authoured several novels, including two major classics of American literature, *The Adventures of Tom Sawyer* and *Adventures of Huckleberry Finn*. Twain was a riverboat pilot, journalist, lecturer, entrepreneur and inventor. He became a national treasure due to his timeless compositions.

When Mark was 4 years old, the Clemens family moved to Hannibal, a bustling town of 1,000 people. John Clemens, Mark's father worked as a storekeeper, lawyer, judge, and land speculator, dreaming of wealth but never achieving it. Sometimes it became hard to even feed his family. John was a serious kind of a person; he never smiled! His mother on the contrary was a fun-loving and tenderhearted homemaker who whiled away many a winter's night for her family by telling them stories. In 1847 when John died unexpectedly, Jane had to take the responsibility of the family. The Clemens family then became almost penniless. They were forced into years of economic struggle — a fact that would shape the career of Mark Twain.

Life in Hannibal

Mark Twain lived in the town of Hannibal from age 4 to age 17. This town, situated on the Mississippi River, was a splendid place in many ways for growing up. Steamboats arrived there three times a day tooting their whistles. There were circuses, minstrel shows, and tradesmen such as blacksmiths and tanners practiced their entertaining crafts there. But in spite of all these positive points, violence was common in the town of Hannibal. Mark had seen many deaths.

Hannibal inspired several of Mark Twain's fictional locations, including 'St. Petersburg' in Tom Sawyer and Huckleberry Finn. These imaginary river towns are portrayed as rather complex places. They were sunny and exuberant on one hand, and on the other hand it was the seat of cruelty, poverty, drunkenness and loneliness. All of this had been a part of Mark's childhood days. Mark could only continue with his schooling upto the age of 12.

Twain's home in Hannibal

After his father's death he found employment as an apprentice printer at the Hannibal Courier. At the age of 15, he got a job as a printer and an occasional writer and editor at the Hannibal Western Union, a little newspaper owned by his brother, Orion.

At the age of 21, Marks began learning the art of piloting a steamboat on the Mississippi. He became a licensed pilot by 1859. He loved his career as it was exciting and well-paying. However, his service was cut short in 1861 by the outbreak of the Civil War, which halted most civilian traffic on the river. As the war began, Mark joined the Confederate

Army in June 1861, but serving for only a couple of weeks until his volunteer unit got disbanded.

In July, Mark headed for Nevada and California, where he lived for the next five years. At first, he tried to earn and save his struggling family. But nothing happened. In September 1862, he went to work as a reporter for the *Virginia City Territorial Enterprise*. He churned out news stories, editorials and sketches. It was then that he adopted the pen name 'Mark Twain'.

In February 1870, Marks improved his social status by marrying 24-year-old Olivia Langdon, the daughter of a rich New York coal merchant.

Mark Twain's family

Twain's Early Compositions

Twain became one of the best known storytellers in the West. He had a distinctive narrative style which was friendly, humourous, often satirical. In 1865, when one of his tales about life in a mining camp, *Jim Smiley and His Jumping Frog*, was printed in the newspapers and magazines around the country, he gained instant fame. His next step up the ladder of success came in 1867, when he took a five-month sea cruise in the Mediterranean, and authoured the book The Innocents Abroad which was published in 1869. This book became an instant bestseller.

The publication of the novel *Adventures of Huckleberry Finn* in England in December 1884, and in the United States in February 1885 created much stirring. Perhaps for the first time in America, the vivid, raw, not-so-respectable voice of the common folk was used to create great literature. *Huck Finn* required years to conceptualize and write. In the meantime, he published *The Prince and the Pauper*, a charming novel. Next, he wrote *Life on the Mississippi*, an interesting travel book.

Twain's next masterpiece *The Adventures of Tom Sawyer* published in the year 1876 was about a young boy growing up along the Mississippi River. The story is set in the background of the town of St. Petersburg, inspired by Hannibal, Missouri, where Mark Twain lived.

Later Works

In 1889, Twain published a novel about ancient England called *A Connecticut Yankee in King Arthur's Court*. His next major work was *The Tragedy of Pudd'nhead Wilson*, a somber novel. He also wrote short stories and essays, and several other books, including a study of Joan of Arc.

Mark Twain's last fifteen years of his life were filled with public honours. He even got degrees from Oxford and Yale. He was photographed and applauded wherever he went probably because he was the most famous American of the late 19th century.

Struggles in Personal Life

While Mark Twain had a life full of recognition and it was gilded with awards, they also brought him much anguish. In his early years of marriage he and his wife lost their toddler son, Langdon to diphtheria. In 1896 his favourite daughter, Susy, died at the age of 24 of spinal meningitis. This shattered Twain. Again, his youngest daughter, Jean, was diagnosed with severe epilepsy in the mid 1890s. In 1909, when she was 29 years old, she died of a heart attack. For many years, Twain's relationship with his middle daughter Clara was distant and full of quarrels. In June 1904, his wife Livy died after a long illness.

Twain became somewhat bitter in his later years. Though he seemed to be an amiable person in public, in private, he was shockingly insensitive to friends and loved ones. His memory faltered. He had volcanic rages and nasty bouts of paranoia. He experienced many periods of depressed indolence too, which he tried to lessen by smoking cigars, reading in bed, and playing hours of billiards and cards.

Mark Twain died at age 74 on April 21, 1910, at his country home in Redding, Connecticut. He was buried in Elmira, New York.

Diphtheria *a highly contagious bacterial disease causing inflammation of the mucous membranes*

Mark Twain was a great humorist and a great storyteller. He has enriched the literature of the world with a gallery of portraits. He was a remarkable observer and a faithful reporter. Mark Twain despised the injustice of slavery and any form of senseless violence.

Redding, Connecticut

Twain is an expert in crafting humorous verse with biting criticism. Through the authentic depiction of his times he caused much controversy and many of his works have been suppressed, censored or banned. He has published more than thirty books,

Humorist *a humorous writer, performer, or an artist*

hundreds of essays, speeches, articles, reviews, and short stories, many still in print today.

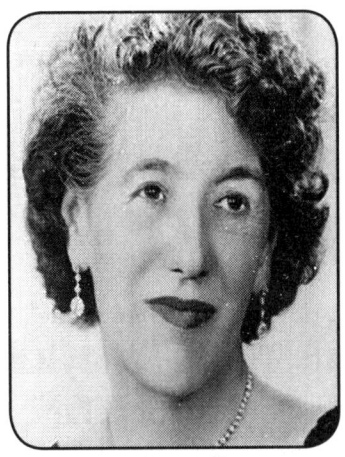

Enid Blyton

Enid Blyton is regarded globally as one of the most successful children's storytellers of the 20th century. She was a British writer rightly described as a 'one-woman fiction machine'. She is noted for numerous series of books designed for different age groups. Her books have enjoyed universal acclaim in many parts of the world, and have sold over 400 million copies. Blyton is the sixth most translated author worldwide!

Early Years

Enid Blyton was born in London, in a small flat above in East Dulwich. She was the eldest of three children. Her father, Thomas Carey Blyton, was multi-talented. He painted in water colours, wrote poetry, learned to play piano, taught himself foreign languages, and was a photographer too. He joined his two older brothers in the family 'mantle warehousing' business after working as a cutlery salesman. Theresa Mary Hamilton, Enid's mother, did not share her husband's interests at all! She did not approve that Enid read books all the time. After Thomas started an affair with another woman, she moved with her children to Beckenham. Thomas established a successful wholesale clothing business in London. He took care of his children's expenses and sent regularly money to support his family. Thomas died in 1920 and Enid did not attend his funeral.

Enid Blyton was very close to her father and spent many hours walking with him in the countryside. The reason behind this special bonding is Enid's love of reading. She exchanged information with her father who was a well-read person. Enid went to St. Christopher's school in Beckenham, where she excelled in sports as well as in academics. This earned her the title of the 'head girl'.

Marriage

In 1924, Blyton married Hugh Pollock, an editor of the book department of George Newnes. None of the members of hers or Pollock's families were present at the wedding cere-mony. In the years 1899 and 1902, the couple was blessed with their sons, Hanley and Carey. In the mid 1930s, Blyton experienced a spiritual crisis. Although, she rarely attended church services, she saw that her two daughters, Gillian and Imogen, were baptized into the Anglican faith and went to the local Sunday School. Blyton being a workaholic, devoted herself to her writing with increased intensity.

Enid with her second husband Kenneth

Blyton's marriage ended in 1942. Next year she married Kenneth Darrell Waters, a middle-aged surgeon. Kenneth was genuinely interested in her work and they shared many interests in common, including gardening.

Enid's Works

Enid had an extraordinary record of publishing over 600 children's or juvenile books during her 40 year career. By the 1980s, Blyton's books had sold some 60 million copies and had been translated into nearly seventy languages!

From her earliest childhood, Blyton had been taught to belief that she would eventually become a musician. However, she had started to write and send stories, articles, and poems to various periodicals. Although, her family thought, that most of her writing was a complete waste of time, Enid remained undaunted. Her first published poem was called *'Have You–?'* which appeared in Nash's Magazine. Blyton's first book was *Child Whispers* which was a collection of poems. This twenty-four-page creation was followed by *Real Fairies: Poems , Responsive Singing Games, The*

Workaholic *a person who works too hard for long hours*
Baptize *the process of admitting someone into Christianity*
Juvenile *a young person*

Enid Blyton Book of Fairies, Songs of Gladness, The Zoo Book, and other books published by J. Saville and Newnes.

Blyton, who was trained to be a kindergarten teacher at Ipswich High School, opened her own infants' school. When her commitments in the literary field increased, Blyton devoted herself entirely to writing. In 1926 Blyton took on editing a new magazine for children, *Sunny Stories for Little People*. Whatever Enid wrote stories, plays, and songs for Teachers' World, were received with great enthusiasm. She also compiled a children's encyclopedia. It was from the 1930s, when her stories began to attract a wider audience.

Enid with her daughters

During World War II, when publishing was restricted, Enid managed to get her works printed, and made her name a brand. In the decades to come she ruled the field of juvenile literature. With her portable typewriter, Blyton could keep up her prodigious output. The secret of this voluminous creative output can be best explained in Enid's own words. She once explained, 'I shut my eyes for a few minutes... I make my mind a blank and wait – and then, as clearly as I would see real children, my characters stand before me in my mind's eye.'

In 1940, eleven books were published under her name, including *The Secret of Spiggy Holes, Twenty-Minute Tales* and *Tales of Betsy May* (both collections of short stories), *The Children of Cherry Tree Farm*, and a story book annual for the News Chronicle. Under the pen name 'Mary Pollock' she wrote *Three Boys and a Circus* and *Children of Kidillin*.

Blyton's first full-length children's book, *The Secret Island*, was published in 1938. This fast-moving story led to the much popular series as *The Famous Five* which was meant for readers between nine and thirteen years, *The Secret Seven*, for readers between eight and nine years, the *Adventure series*, the *Mystery* series, and the *'Barney' Mystery books*. Enid created young characters who are courageous and resourceful, who encountered adventures without having adults near them. Nevetheless, *The Famous Five* remains her most famous series amongst all. Its central characters were Julian, Dick, Anne, George, and the dog Timmy.

Enid Blyton Magazine which was initiated in 1953 raised money for children who had spastic cerebral palsy. Another very renowned series *Little Noddy Goes to Toyland* is a story of a little toy man, who always landed up in troubles and had to seek help from his Toyland friends. This book was a huge success. Other Noddy books of various sizes and types followed in rapid succession. 'Noddy' became a household name. The series also produced a play and a film.

Last Life and Death

In the early sixties, Blyton's memory began to fail and she probably was affected by Alzheimer's disease though it was kept a secret. Blyton found it increasingly difficult to write. *Five Are Together Again* (1963) was the last in the 'famous five' series. Her husband died in 1967. After her husband's death, Blyton's illness grew worse. And finally she died in her sleep on November 28, 1968, in a Hampsted nursing home.

Criticism of Blyton's Works

Blyton was the most prolific children's writer in the post-war period. In the 1950s and 1960s her books were attacked from many sides. BBC had kept her work off air until 1963. Librarians imposed sanctions on her publications as they thought that her works had very limited vocabulary. But the main target of criticism revolved around the character of Noddy. Rumours were spread that she did not write all her own books. Although her books were criticized for racism and snobbishness, they always found new readers from new generations. In the words of psychologist Michael Woods, *'She was a* child, she thought as a child and she wrote as a child.' This opinion actually summarizes Blyton's secret of success.

It was long believed that there are no more unpublished or unknown Blyton works waiting to be discovered, until a 180 page fantasy novel, titled *Mr Trumpy's Caravan*, was found in 2011. Critics have often criticized that Enid used the same plot over and over again. Blyton was also severely criticised, because she seemed to have said that the opinions of people over 12 didn't matter to her at all!

Enid Blyton's Best Selling Books

In a span of 40 years, Enid Blyton wrote about 800 books! The most popular series among them are:

- *The Magic Faraway Tree series*
- *The Barney Mystery series*
- *The Mystery series*
- *The Malory Towers series*
- *The Famous Five series*
- *The Amelia Jane short stories*

Snobbishness *an attitude in which a rich person treats others with contempt*

- *The Secret Seven series*
- *The St. Clare's series*
- *The Wishing-Chair series*
- *The Naughtiest Girl series*
- *The Willow Farm series*

Even though critics found many flaws in her work, Enid Blyton never failed to enthrall her young readers. She truly was a writer for the children.

J.K. Rowling

J.K. Rowling is the much recognized British author who gained global attention for her Harry Potter series. Her best-selling novels have sold more than 400 million copies and won numerous awards. The books have also been adapted to screen in a series of blockbuster films. Rowling has been ranked as the twelfth richest woman in the United Kingdom in 2008 with a net worth of US$1 billion! She is often said to have risen from 'rags to riches'.

Birth and Early Years

Joanne Kathleen Rowling popularly called J.K Rowling was born on July 31, 1965, in Chipping Sodbury, near Bristol, England. Rowling was a single mother living in Edinburgh, Scotland. She became an international literary sensation in 1999, when the first three installments of her Harry Potter came on the top three slots of The New York Times best-seller list. When the fourth volume in the series was published in 2000, *Harry Potter and the Goblet of Fire*, it became the fastest-selling book in history!

Rowling was a graduate of Exeter University. She moved to Portugal in 1990 to teach English. There, she met and married the Portuguese journalist Jorge Arantes. The couple's daughter, Jessica, was born in 1993. But sadly, the marriage did not last for long. After her marriage ended in a divorce, Rowling moved to Edinburgh with her daughter to live near her younger sister, Di. Life as a single mother was difficult in the bleak Scottish winter. Rowling was diagnosed with clinical depression due to which she even contemplated committing

Contemplated to think deeply or to look at something thoughtfully

suicide. While struggling to support Jessica and herself on welfare, Rowling struck upon the idea of writing which had occurred to her while she was travelling on a train from Manchester to London in 1990.

Rising to Fame and Recognition

The recognition for Rowling's work with the creation of the character of Harry Potter did not bring overnight fame and fortune to the author. In 1995, she finished typing out 'Harry Potter and the Philosopher's Stone' on an old manual typewriter, and sent it out to various literary agents. A reader called Bryony Evans, at Christopher Little literary agents, at once recognised the potential of her work. And so, the firm promptly agreed to represent her, sending the book out to at least twelve publishers. Rowling had to wait patiently for a whole year before she found a publisher. The lucky firm which was the small publishing house of Bloomsbury gained unthinkable fame after publishing her work. There is a publishing legend that the decision to publish the book owes much to Alice Newton, the eight-year-old daughter of Bloomsbury's chairman!

And so, Rowling's first book *Harry Potter and the Philosopher's Stone* (later the word 'Philosopher' was changed to 'Sorcerer') was published in June 1997, with an initial print run of one thousand copies, 500 of which were sold to libraries. The book, and its subsequent series, chronicled the life of Harry Potter, a young wizard, and his multi-coloured band at the Hogwarts School of Witchcraft and Wizardry. These initial copies of Harry Potter books are now regarded as collector's items, and are estimated to be worth up to £25,000 apiece!

Rowling at a book launch

Wizard *a man from the fairy tales having magical powers*

As her books gained more exposure, Rowling's talent and ability as a children's writer became more established. Later books like *Harry Potter and the Chamber of Secrets, Harry Potter and the Prisoner of Azkaban, Harry Potter and the Goblet of Fire* and the others were published. One of the first Awards she won was the much-coveted 'Nestle Smarties Award'. She won the award three consecutive times, before thoughtfully withdrawing her fourth book, in order to give the other writers a chance to compete. A grant of £8,000 from the Scottish Arts Council enabled her to carry on writing full-time.

In 1998, one short year after her first book had seen print, she sold the film rights for her first two books to Warner Brothers which made her a millionaire overnight. When her fourth book, *'Harry Potter and the Goblet of Fire'* was published, the book broke all previous publishing records in the United Kingdom and United States. Rowling was named 'Author of The Year' at the British Book Awards in 2000.

Charities and Working for Causes

Rowling, is now Britain's 13th wealthiest woman—wealthier than even the Queen! She has used her considerable wealth and power to establish herself as a notable philanthropist. In 2000, she founded the 'Volant Charitable Trust', which sets aside £5.1 million annually to help women and children in need. She is also the President of the charitable organization 'One Parent Families now called 'Gingerbread'. In 2005, Rowling co-founded the Children's High Level Group', which aims to make life better for young people in care in Eastern Europe, and ultimately all over the world. In February 2010, this charity became 'Lumos'. Since 1999, Rowling has been a supporter of the 'Multiple Sclerosis Society', Scotland. Although she has recently stepped down as Patron of the charity, she continues to fund MS research directly.

Personal Life

In December 2001, Rowling married Neil Michael Murray, an anaesthetist, in a private ceremony at her home in Aberfeldy, Scotland. The couple was blessed with a son David Gordon Rowling Murray,

Rowling and Neil Michael

in March 2003. In January 2005, she gave birth to a daughter, Mackenzie Jean.

Beyond Harry Potter

Having completed the final installment of the seventh book of the Harry Potter series which was published in July 2007, Rowling has disclosed that she is not planning to write an eighth book. In her own words she said, *'In ten years time, I might want to return to it, but I think it's unlikely.'* She also said that she wanted to spend a lot of good, quality time with her family, but would continue writing for children because that's what she enjoyed. *The Tales of Beedle the Bard* was published in December 2008. Since that time, Rowling has turned her attention to adult literature. On April 12, 2012, she revealed the title of her new book 'A Casual Vacancy'.

Honours and Awards

- J K Rowling was voted 'Author of the Year' at the 1999 British Book Awards

- 'Author of the Year' award by The Booksellers Association consecutively for two years

- She won the 'W H Smith Children's Book of the Year' for 2000 and in 2004

- Was awarded the WH Smith's 'Fiction Award'

- In 2006, won the Nibbie's (Children's Book of the Year) for *Harry Potter and the Half-Blood Prince.*

- Received the 2008 British Book 'Awards' Lifetime Achievement Award'

- In 2001, received the 'Order of the British

Empire' (OBE) from His Royal Highness the Prince of Wales, for services to children's literature

- In 2003, received Spain's prestigious 'Prince of Asturias Award for Concord'

- In February 2009, she was inducted into France's prestigious 'Legion of Honor' and given the honorary title of 'knight'

- Honorary degrees were bestowed from Harvard University, Dartmouth College, New Hampshire USA, University of Exeter, University of St Andrews, Napier University, Edinburgh, and University of Edinburgh

Rowling at an Award Ceremony

Critics on Rowling

Rowling is praised for her highly imaginative and creative talent. Her work possesses intricate plots, and she is often compared to authors like Roald Dahl, P. L. Travers and C. S. Lewis. It has been noticed by critics and readers alike that Rowling has the ability to use interesting words and names in her books. Many a time critics comment that the plots of the first three books are rather formulaic, nevertheless they are highly entertaining and worth reading. One of the most striking things about Rowling's works is the amount of excitement they have generated. In spite of a few negative opinions, overall, the series has received the support of parents, teachers and librarians. J. K Rowling is read, loved and respected by children and adult alike since the time she has begun writing.

LEWIS CARROLL

The most striking quality of Lewis Carroll maybe that he was a person divided between a prim and pedantic mathematician and a delightful writer of children's stories!

Birth and Early Life

Charles Lutwidge Dodgson or Lewis Carroll (pen name) was an English logician, mathematician, photographer, and novelist, best known for his fantasy, *Alice in Wonderland*.

Dodgson was the eldest son and the third child in a family of seven girls and four boys. His mother was Frances Jane Lutwidge, the wife of the Reverend Charles Dodgson. Dodgson was born in Daresbury, Cheshire, on January 27, 1832.

His family lived in an isolated country village and had few friends outside the family. But they found little difficulty in entertaining themselves as Charles always invented games to amuse them. The Rectory Magazines, manuscript compilations to which his family was supposed to contribute, were created when Charles was 12. The Rectory Magazine was one of several family publications that Lewis Carroll edited, wrote for, and illustrated (with some contributions from his brothers and sisters) during his teens. It was a blend of prose, verse, satiric reviews, and illustrations. The Rectory Magazine revealed a lot of intelligence and wit. In fact, Charles wrote nearly all of the surviving text.

The young adult Charles Dodgson was about six feet tall, thin and fairly handsome, with curly brown hair and blue eyes. At the age of seventeen, he suffered a severe attack of whooping cough which left Charles with poor hearing in his right ear. He also suffered from a problem of stammering which he had acquired in his early childhood. This problem was to plague him throughout his life. It is often claimed that Charles only stammered in the company of adults, and was free and fluent with children!

As a child, Charles attended the Richmond School, Yorkshire from 1844-45, and then Rugby School from 1846-50. After Rugby he spent a year being tutored by his father, during which he matriculated from Christ Church, Oxford. Charles excelled in mathematics and divinity studies in the year 1852. On the basis of his performance in examinations, he was

Richmond School

nominated to a studentship (called a scholarship in other colleges).

Although, Charles has often been described as 'shy', he does not in reality seem to have been so. In fact, he seemed to have been quite socially active. He could sing quite well and never hesitated to do so in public. He was even good at mimicry and, of course, story telling. Though often described in biographies as hardworking, in reality his early academic career was very uneven. Due to his own laziness he failed an important scholarship. This is a fact which he himself confessed. But his brilliance as a mathematician won him the Christ Church Mathematical Lectureship, which he continued to hold for the next 26 years.

Charles had an inclination for writing from his early adolescence if not before. He wrote poetry, short stories for his family magazines, and by the mid 1850s he began sending his work to various magazines, consequently enjoying moderate success. Between the years 1954 and 1956, his work appeared in the national publications, The Comic Times and The Train, as well as smaller magazines like the Whitby Gazette and the Oxford Critic. Most of his output was comic, sometimes sharply satirical.

In addition to his writing pursuits, he loved the theatre and the arts. In the year 1856, he took up photography which was to be a passion for him for the next 24 years. According to his biographer and nephew Stuart Collingwood, young Charles began to keep a diary almost as soon as he could write. In the year 1853, Charles began a new series of numbered diary volumes which he continued to keep until his death, and most of these do survive.

His Works

Before the publication of the two Alices, Charles had published a number of humorous items in verse and prose and a few serious poems. The earliest works appeared anonymously, but in March 1856 a poem called *Solitude* was published using the pseudonym Lewis Carroll. This name was used later for all his works as an author and a poet.

Creating his Masterpieces—Alice in Wonderland and its Sequel

It has been observed that Charles had a strong affinity for children. Charles loved to entertain children. And it was Alice, the daughter of Henry George Liddell, who can be credited to have inspired him to create his best work, *Alice in Wonderland*. Alice Liddell remembers that she used to spend many hours with Charles, sitting on his couch while he told fantastic tales of dream worlds to her. One day, during an afternoon picnic with Alice and her two sisters Lorina and Edith, Charles told the first rough draft of what would later become *Alice's Adventures in Wonderland*. When little Alice arrived home, she exclaimed that he must write the story down for her.

Charles fulfilled the little girl's request. Through a series of coincidences, the story fell into the hands of the novelist Henry Kingsley, who urged Charles to publish it. And that's how the book *Alice's Adventures in Wonderland* was released in 1865. It was hugely applauded and it gained steady popularity. And as a result, Carroll wrote

sequel *a published or recorded work that continues a story*

the sequel, *Through the Looking-Glass and What Alice Found There* in 1871. By the time of his death, Alice had become the most popular children's book in England, and by 1932 it was one of the most popular and talked about book in the world.

Alice Liddell

Dodgson remained at Christ Church for the next thirty-six years when his wealth and fame increased considerably. After the death of his father in 1868, Charles went into depression. In 1872 came his great mock-epic *The Hunting of the Snark*, in 1876, and his last novel the two volumes *Sylvie and Bruno*. He also published many mathematical papers under his own name and toured Russia and Europe. His journal of the trip was published years after his death. Charles had also authored a number of books on mathematics though none of enduring importance.

Photography and Carroll

Carroll is also remembered as a fine photographer of children and of adults as well. Portraits of the actress Ellen Terry, the poet Alfred Lord Tennyson, the poet-painter Dante Gabriel Rossetti, and many others have survived and have been often reproduced. However, in 1880 Dodgson abandoned his hobby altogether, as he started feeling that it was taking up too much time that might be better spent.

A little before his 66th birthday, Lewis Carroll suffered from a severe fit of influenza, which led to pneumonia. He died on January 14, 1898, leaving behind him his immortal works.

Critical Comments

Carroll's publications particularly the Alice stories were enormously popular with juvenile readers. They have been reprinted countless times and have been translated into virtually every modern language. The two books were originally considered 'nonsense' for the amusement of children. They were considered not to be taken very seriously and hence were never analyzed by serious scholars. In the 1930s, however, the Alice stories and the nonsense poem *The Hunting of the Snark* had attracted increasing attention from literary critics and philosophers. Many critics reject the idea that Carroll was a nonsense writer and claim that the author should be more properly categorized as an 'absurdist'.

Whatever the critics' opinion, Carroll's Alice books have become timeless over the years. They are read, enjoyed and appreciated even till today.

AGATHA CHRISTIE

Agatha Christie was the best-selling mystery writer of all times. She was popularly called the 'Queen of Crime'. She wrote 93 books and 17 plays, including the longest-running play of modern day theater, *The Mousetrap*. She is the only mystery writer to have created two important detectives as characters, Hercule Poirot and Miss Marple.

Childhood and Family

Agatha Mary Clarissa Miller was born at Torquay in the United Kingdom on September 15, 1890. Her father Frederick Alvah Miller was an American and her mother Clara Boehmer was an English. She was the youngest of the three children. Her brother was called Monty and sister, Madge.

On October 20 in 1890, she was baptized in the church. All Saints' Church, which was about a twenty minute walk from their house. There is quite a bit of history behind her name! She received her name Mary after her grandmother, Clarissa after her mother and Agatha after a suggestion by a friend on a way to the church.

Agatha spent her childhood at Ashfield, in a Victorian villa which she loved and which had a very strong influence on her life. Her family was comfortable financially, although not wealthy. She didn't go to any formal

Young Agatha

school but was educated at home. From the beginning, Agatha was a bright child, who taught herself to read by the age of five. She liked reading and she also took piano, singing, dancing, and tennis lessons.

She grew up in an environment which was full of stories. Her mother narrated tales full of drama and suspense. And her elder sister told her frightening tales. Agatha began creating her own fictions, with the help of her nanny, her dolls, and her pets. When she was only 11 years old, her father died. At the age of sixteen she was sent to Paris where she learnt to sing and to play the piano. She considered becoming a professional opera singer but her voice was not strong enough. Next, she thought of becoming a concert pianist but her music teacher told her that she was too nervous to play in front of an audience. Nevertheless, she continued to play privately at Greenway House and elsewhere.

In the year 1914, Christie married Archibald Christie, an officer in the Flying Royal Corps. Rosalind their daughter, was born in 1919. During World War I, she worked in a Red Cross Hospital in Torquayas as a hospital dispenser, which gave her a knowledge of poisons. This knowledge was particularly useful when she started developing the plots of her mysteries. The couple moved into a house called 'Styles' after her first novel. But unfortunately, their marriage was unhappy. It didn't last because Archie had fallen in love with another woman and had asked for a divorce in 1926. In this year, Agatha's mother too passed away.

Agatha with her Second Husband

She suffered such a mental breakdown that on December 6, she disappeared from her home suddenly. Her car was found abandoned in a quarry. Ten days later, the police found her in a hotel in Harrogate, England. Strangely, she had been staying the entire time, registered under the name of the woman with whom her husband was having an affair! Agatha claimed to have had amnesia (severe memory loss), and so, the case was not pursued further. She divorced her first husband two years later.

In 1930 Christie married Sir Max Mallowan, a leading British archaeologist. She often went with him on his expeditions to Iraq and Syria. As a result, she placed some of her novels in those countries. In *Come, Tell Me How You Live* (1946) she wrote a humorous account of some of her travels with her husband. Agatha's sense of humour can be seen through her comment about her husband in which she said, *'An archaeologist is the best husband any woman can have. The older she gets, the more interested he is in her.'*

Works

The year 1926 was important for Christie for another important reason apart from the tragedies she went through. It saw the publication of her first hugely successful novel, *The Murder of Roger Ackroyd*, in which the narrator is the murderer.

Agatha at Work

Christie's first detective novel, *The Mysterious Affair at Styles*, introduced **Hercule Poirot**, the Belgian detective, who appeared in more than

40 books, the last of which was *Curtain* (1975). Undoubtedly, one of the most captivating fictional creations of all times, Poirot's 'little grey cells' always triumphed over horrible criminals in 33 novels and many dozens of short stories. Christie's last published novel, *Sleeping Murder* in 1976, featured her other world-famous detective, the shrewdly inquisitive **Miss Jane Marple** of St. Mary Mead. Miss Marple appeared in twelve novels, beginning with *The Murder at the Vicarage* in 1930.

Both Hercule Poirot and Miss Marple have been widely dramatized in feature films and television shows. *Murder on the Orient Express, Witness for the Prosecution, And Then There Were None, and Death on the Nile* are a few of the successful films based on her works.

In a writing career that spanned more than half a century, Agatha Christie wrote 79 novels and short stories. She also wrote over a dozen plays including *The Mousetrap*, which opened in London in November in the year 1952.

Agatha Christie also wrote six romantic novels under the pen name, Mary Westmacott. She wrote four books including an autobiography and an entertaining account of the numerous archeological expeditions she shared with her second husband, Sir Max Mallowan. In the year 1971, Agatha achieved her country's highest honour when she received the 'Order of Dame Commander of the British Empire'.

Agatha Christie died on January 12 , 1976. Her demise caused a great loss to the world of suspense literature. Agatha Christie remains unparalleled even till today. She is a master of suspense, plotting, and characterisation.